Tears in Translation

Carmen King

BookLeaf Publishing

India | USA | UK

Presentation by *BookLeaf Publishing*

Web: www.bookleafpub.com

E-mail: info@bookleafpub.com

ISBN: 9789360944469

First edition 2024

This is dedicated to the Ones I Love

ACKNOWLEDGEMENT

I want to thank my dear husband, who so graciously gives me the space to be obedient to my call. My children, who have been instrumental in giving me something to write about.

PREFACE

In 2009 A woman of faith told me that there was a writer inside of me. This was strange to me because I had only been writing resumes and obituaries, and did not actually consider that writing. Over the years the revelation of her words were shown to be true and I began to put my thoughts and feelings on paper. This is part of my story in poem.

Oh Mother

Young and alone,
didn't even know what was going on,
but the baby must live on!
Through tears and fears, she came.
Regular girl regular name.

Oh Mother!
How alone you must have been,
how cold you must have felt.
The pain you had to endure with no one to hold
your hand.

Oh Mother!
What strength it must have took,
what courage in your heart!
What love it must have been to push out a new
start.

Oh Mother!
The love that filled the air,
the warmth that shattered the cold,
the pain you no longer bear,
the hand you now have to hold!

Oh Mother!

You endured that all for me,
a child that still must grow.
You gave your life, your love, and your liberty
although others said, "NO"!

For this, for my life,
words will not suffice,
so I'll just say, "I love you"!

Oh Mother!

The Beat Of My Heart

The beat of my heart and the course of my
thoughts lead me on a never-ending journey.
The footsteps of my mind leave imprints on
paper, filling it with overwhelming emotion.
From out of a deep pit of darkness, light flows,
healing and revealing all that is within.
I write!

Words trek across my inner sanctum and engulf
me with understanding.
I am now radiant!
The riches and depths of treasures unseen pass
through me.
Covered in peace that surpasses my
understanding,
content with what is and faith filled with what
shall be!
I write I write!

These words have now taken on the guise of a
vision, manifestation is now eminent!
I can see the glow and how the words now flow,
bringing me to a place never seen with the eye
of my mind.

I smile because the words that swirl around
inside no longer hide in the recesses of my heart!
I am free to be me!
There is no shame in the words that have come
from life in the mundane!
I write I write I write!

Death To Self

I've known her all my life, and now she must
face a great sacrifice.

This is a journey dark and deep.
Where decisions are made beyond wisdom's
reach.

Her pain, my pain,
her fear, my fear,
her joy, my joy.

I love her and sleep with her,
even cry and laugh with her.

This is a terror I've never felt before,
in its grip, I'm lost, uncertain and sore.

I've tied myself to her for a very long time,
now this rope I must unwind.
She has to die, she must go,
before darkness covers her final glow.

If I keep her here with me,
there will be a life I never see.
Far beyond the reaches of my imagination,

lies a world awaiting my exploration.
But I must do it alone, on my won, without her.

Self must die and secrets kept.

Surrendered to the greater whole,
I found redemption for my weary soul.

In letting go true freedom's found.
Death to self, a paradox profound.

What will be said when she is found dead?
I don't know, but I've go to let her go.

There's a new woman on the horizon
and my God is smilin'!

For I have found life out of death!

Blood On My Hands

Time slips by, a relentless tide, and fate's decree
we cannot hide.

Your tears flowed with silent pain,
and I failed to utter His sacred name.
Your plea to Heaven, so close, so clear,
yet I hesitated, gripped by fear.

The mention of His name carries the balm to
heal, your shattered pieces begin to seal.
To help you gather the scattered shards
and mend the rift, the battle scars.

To put together what once was whole,
to nurture hope within your soul.
The mention of His name gathers every care,
and to this I was fully aware.

Your BLOOD now staining my trembling hands,
a mark of regret, where conscience stands.
I bear this burden, this weight, this shame,
for love unspoken, a silent blame.

On that dark night, as you took flight, did you
find solace in His light?

Your BLOOD upon my hands, a stark affair,
a constant reminder of love I didn't share.
Your memory a beacon to bear, forever there,
in the stain upon my hands.

For others now, my heart does care,
to spread the truth, this love to share.
That the one who reigns can mend the fray,
wash away sorrow, brighten the day.

In His embrace, all brokenness finds ease,
in His love, every burden flees.
Regardless of the mess we've made,
His grace, unyielding, will never fade.

A poem for Darryl

Section 12 Row 22

As I watch the Weeping Willow tree blow in the
wind, and feel its breath upon my skin,
it whispers your name in my ear.
Blowing memories of you through the corners of
my mind.
I smell the freshness of pine,
that only the deep south can deliver.
Moving through the grass, now brown from
winters hush,
I look down.
Tears flowed at the reality of what I was seeing.
A headstone, so hard, so cold, with your name
written in bold.
Desiree Marie King!

I cannot believe how real this is.
Realer than the day we brought you here,
is the day I stand here 7 years later.

I did not know that the cold tears flowing down
my cheeks would cool the warmth of the sun
shining on my face.

As much as I want to leave,
it's hard to go.

It feels like I'm leaving you behind,
just as I did the first time.
Wishing you could come with me is only a wish.

So I'll bid you farewell, in the silence deep,
and let you rest, in the arms of gentle sleep.

Church Folks

In the flickers of my imagination,
I see Jesus moving through His earth,
a massive garden,
a display of His splendor.

The time for inspection is at hand,
has the church been diligent with His plan?

This massive garden, filled with all species of
flowering plants.
He moves with precision and quietness.
A quietness that awaits the garden's fate.

His hand gently sweeps across each plant.
Inspecting every root, stem and flower with
wisdom that only belongs to the Master Gardner.
The constitution of the soil, its vitality and
appearance,
looked over with due diligence.
I watch the Master skillfully touch each bloom,
not to harm it or to bring its doom.

He seeks to feel the essence of what runs
through the recesses of the soil,
that fill the deep roots below,

and penetrate its life flow.

He turns towards me,
there is a tear in His eye that I can see.
Now the silence that once hovered,
is lost in the deep as the Master speaks.

You've wrapped me in a dialogue that isn't mine,
your feet tarry where I am not, and your hands
no longer do my bidding.
WHERE ARE YOU AND WHO ARE YOU
WITH?

I strained for your voice, but heard no reply.
In the vast expanse, you seemed to hide.
WHERE ARE YOU AND WHO ARE YOU
WITH?

Through fields I wandered, eyes keen and
yearning,
yet found no soul, no presence discerning.
In the empty fields, there was no laboring hand.
WHERE ARE YOU AND WHO ARE YOU
WITH?

Courage falters, strength deceives,
wisdom eludes, zeal takes leave.
WHERE ARE YOU AND WHO ARE YOU
WITH?

Lost in shadows, seeking a myth,
I am not happy; I find no pleasure in this!

WHERE ARE YOU AND WHO ARE YOU
WITH!

Unbound

Echoes of the past,
I step forward, free of chains,
today I choose light!

Rest

Heart's beat gently hums,
mind finds peace in silent night,
sleep's embrace arrives.

Winter's Reason

The warm breeze glides through the trees as the
sun ascends to its designated place.
The brown leaves crunch under my steady pace
and speaks so loudly of what's to come.

You know the one...
The one who wraps me in its coldness and
refuses to let me go.
The pain of you,
my disdain for you.
Shutting me in without a care.
Why do you have to come?

Covering me in blankets of your thickness,
your carpet, wet and cold.
Your dreariness causes my weariness.
I see no need for you here,
your purpose is quite unclear.
Why do you have to come?

What is that you say?
Rest for the earth is why you stay.
The needed withdrawal of sunlight and heat is
essential for renewal in earth's time of retreat.

So be not so quick to shun the darkness that
covers and cools,
for it offers rest to renew.
Wrap up in its stillness and silence,
and welcome the enriching aspects of winter's
long plight.

For this is a season of preparation for days soon
filled with light.

Ruth And Naomi

I've heard this story a thousand times.
Studied it in Sunday school and even heard it
preached,
and I only understood with my mind.
Now because of you I understand it in my heart.

See, you've shown me your God in such a
simple way.
A mirror of His loving kindness and gentleness,
you are.
The flow of tender mercies that pour from your
heart,
I see why Ruth followed and would not, could
not turn away.

We've talked, laughed, and cried,
and the light that shines from your heart has
never died.
Your selfless love, so reflective of your Father's
heart.
I see why Ruth followed and would not, could
not turn away.

This simply leads me to say...
I'll be your Ruth if you'll be my Naomi.

A poem for my Mother-in-Love

Petitions

Crackers no chaser is like
Bread and no water.
This is how our lips feel when we see our
daughters being led to slaughter!

Our voices are lifted steadfast and strong.
In this journey, fraught with trials untold,
we fight from a place...
our anchored souls.

Cracker crumbs scattered,
prayers and pain for our kin,
hopes of seeing their trials come to an end.

Dry mouths parched with cries.
Will the Lord quench our longing?

Though our mouths are dry and voices weak,
it matters not,
for in faith we pray,
their resolve we seek.

In the end, we will win
If we keep on praying!

How To Be A Boss

Listen young one,
put down your gun
and pick up your cross
that's how you become a boss.

Thorns on His head.
He bled, died and said,
I do this in your stead.

Listen young one,
put down your gun
and pick up your cross
that's how you become a boss.

Now you're
afraid to sleep and
afraid to eat.
You didn't know your conscience would creep
into the seams of your dreams,
and cause a current in your soul that nearly takes
its toll.
Without it being said,
you're really the one that's dead.

LISTEN YOUNG ONE,

PUT DOWN YOUR GUN.
PICK UP YOUR CROSS AND BE A REAL
BOSS!

Word For Life

Life be lifing, so it is said.
Its rhythms and rhymes,
it ebbs and flows,
the way it sometimes takes,
you'll never know.
I've found a way to seize the day...I fill myself
with words of wisdom.
The confessions of my mouth spring forth from
my heart.
In words, find solace,
in language find might.

Do your words ring deep and true in the tapestry
of life?
For in the shaping of our speech we find our
way,
to navigate the challenges of another day.

So make your words strong...
a torrent of truth, a creative art,
forging a path into wisdom's heart.

Great Awakening

The greatest weights we seem not to carry,
leaning on You becomes an easy thing to do.

I find the little things are too heavy to bear.
They constantly gnaw at your character,
trying to break you, slowly, slowly, slowly,
until you crack from the weight of its pressure.

The very things I feel I can handle,
are the things where I see,
I need You the most.

Give me strength to bear the little things.
Big or small God wants them all!

Life In A Fog

Can you see through the grime,
can you hear, despite the noise,
can you come out if there is no door?

Why wake with no purpose,
why trample underfoot those that love you,
no matter what it took?

God is in full authority,
His chastening you must allow.
Death has no sting for the grave is disallowed.

Be forever mindful, God is not dead.
He will surely bring to pass all that He said.

Rise out of the mire,
step into the way of the everlasting Christ,
author and finisher of faith!

Fractured

My tears flow within me because my heart is
fractured.
The prideful essence of one, and the pain woven
in the countenance of the other.
The silence is deafening, it is as a cloak worn
upon feeble shoulders.
The air is thick and suffocating.
WHO DON'T BELIEVE IN ENERGY?

Words not expressed is like a broken bone trying
to heal on its own.
Will it ever be the same?
The pain is projected onto the innocent, which
you will one day have to explain.

The other hearts are casualties of their war.
Arrows flying amongst the innocent, seemingly
injuring those that stood in the crossfire of
words and uncontrolled emotions.
No one is truly happy,
no one has truly been made whole.
Each one dives deeper into their own thoughts
and actions,
NOT GOD'S, just theirs.

The divide becomes greater, wider, more
expansive,
filled with lies and treachery.
The bridge is burning on both ends.

And all the fractured one can do is pray.
ALL THE FRACTURED ONE CAN DO IS
PRAY!
ALL THE FRACTURED ONE CAN DO IS
PRAY!

Penning this doesn't relieve my sorrow nor heal
my fracture.
It simply leaves tracks of the past others can
view.

ALL THE FRACTURED ONE CAN DO IS
PRAY!

A heart surrendered to God truly hurts and cries
because of the pain and ignorance of others.
Although it's not my cross to bear, it is my
prayer to bear!

Lord, close the divide, heal the broken hearted,
enlighten the ignorant, protect the innocent and
repair the injuries of those wounded in the
crossfire.

Grave Clothes

What do you do when she enters tattered?
The world has swallowed her, as you knew it
would.
Now regurgitating her, spitting her out.
Leaving her without a breath of hope,
lifeless, tattered and torn.
No Worries though, it's the perfect attire for
deliverance.

She was once wrapped in shrouds, her heart
confined,
in whispers lost, in chains entwined.
Her love, once bright, now draped in gray,
bound by threads of yesterday.
Love was never meant to dwell in tombs of
discontent.

Unbind her and let her go,
it's her time to come out of those grave clothes!
When bonds released, her freedom will flow,
and we'll watch her spirit rise and grow.

She'll hear her name and release the shame of
echoes from her past.

The memories fade and the vibrant flame of love
anew is burning.
From inside she no longer hides,
for the glow of her worth is showing.

For God has called her name and set her free,
just by whispering, "Come forth," to thee.

She was wearing the perfect attire for
deliverance.

Talitha Cumi (Young Girl Rise)

It's not the first time a messy life appears,
leaving muddy footsteps in its wake.
Trapped in trenches of shame and disgust, to
embarrassed to move on.

I moved across the room and embraced her.

Come on in once again, and have a seat at the
table.
I have a friend, and to His love there is no end,
I believe you might even know Him.

He's the one who erased the slate long ago, so
there's no need to worry,
JUST LET GO!

I'm here with you now, just hold my hand,
as I express to you the love of a greater man.
His love will embrace you no matter what.
Your shame, I wipe away,
I clean you off from the muddy clay.
I'll pull you up out of the trench.
You, nor I or anyone can smell the stench.
I'll hold your hand and guide you through,

tears you'll shed, but it no longer hurts to.

I'll encourage you through the dark night,
until you find rest in His peaceful light.
You'll come to know that there is a new day.

As I saw you battered, torn and worn, I waited
patiently.
I'm glad you're here now, a place where I'll
always be.

Your friend,
Grace

Dichotomies Of Life

Shadows dance with light, day and night.
Lows and highs,
truths and falsehood intertwine.

In every loss a gain appears.
In every silence, echoes scream.

The familiar stranger,
goes unseen,
noticed me from afar.

This is clearly, unclear.

GREATNESS

Give glory to God for the greatness in me,
because He that is in me is He that is greater
than He that is in the world!

Ready set go, in a new direction, receive His
correction, love and protection, because He that
is in me is greater than He that is in the world!

Exuberant am I because of the excellence of my
God and knowing that, He that is in me is
greater than He that is in the world!

Allowing God to move me towards my purpose,
because He that is in me is greater than He that
is in the world!

Truth, God's word is the standard for it all, Jesus
Christ is the way the truth and the life. He that is
in me is greater than He that is in the world!

Now is the time to awake, not to break, because
He that is in me is greater than He that is in the
world!

Everlasting, eternal, ever ready to give an
answer for the hope that lies within me, because
He that is in me is greater than He that is in the
world!

Salt of the earth, rebirth, dressed ready for the
battle, because He that is in me is greater than
He that is in the world!

Stand for justice, greatness is inside of me, as I
strive to bless thee, He that is in me is greater
than He that is in the world!

Searching

Where do we find love amidst a sea of hate?
Even though our hearts are scarred with wounds,
love whispers softly to resume.
Overtime our grief will unwind and love will
show up again.
It will heal the fractured parts of our hearts like a
balm on dry skin.

The little flame that flickers in our soul will be
ignited again.
And we'll find peace amidst this beast we call
home.
In the meantime we'll try to find, a reason to
resume.

To resume a life when love found its way
through the noise of fury and hate.
To resume a life where kindness mends callous
words,
and you live like you know love is a verb.

We'll resume the laughter and hope it comes
faster than the next call to the next of kin.
One thing I know about love though...
When it's real it never ends!

That's God's love and it never fails!